S0-BCX-858

FABULOUS FLORIDA

FABULOUS FLORIDA

B.J. Bergman-Angstadt

PREMIUM PRESS AMERICA
NASHVILLE, TENNESSEE

FABULOUS FLORIDA by B.J. Bergman-Angstadt

Published by PREMIUM PRESS AMERICA

Copyright © 1999 PREMIUM PRESS AMERICA

All rights reserved. No part of this book may be reproduced or transmitted in any form or by any means, electronic or mechanical, including photocopying, recording, or by any information storage and retrieval system, without prior written permission of the Publisher, except where permitted by law.

ISBN 1-887654-28-3

Library of Congress Catalog Card Number 97-76473

PREMIUM PRESS AMERICA gift books are available at special discounts for premiums, sales promotions, fund-raising, or educational use. For details contact the Publisher at P.O. Box 159015, Nashville, TN 37215, or phone toll free (800) 891-7323 or (615)256-8484, or fax us at (615)256-8624.

For more information visit our web site at *www.premiumpress.com.*

Editor Mardy Fones
Cover and Interior Design by Bob Bubnis/BookSetters—bksetters@aol.com
Printed by Vaughan Printing

First Edition 1999
1 2 3 4 5 6 7 8 9 10

Acknowledgements

Many thanks to my friends at *Florida Today*, especially Barbara Caywood and the sports staff.

Dedication

To my fabulously supportive husband, Bruce and kids, Ed, Christy and David.

INTRODUCTION

When my father was three years old, his father packed up the family and left Ocilla, Ga., in search of a job on Henry Flagler's railroad. Several years later, my mother's family left Brooklyn, looking for warmer weather, and moved into a house across the street from my father's in the sleepy town of Miami.

By this time, the Depression was in full swing. My paternal grandfather had been laid-off from the railroad and was driving a touring car, toting such notables as Al Capone around the city. My father supplemented his roofing income by coaching tennis. His prize pupil was famed female athlete, Babe Didrikson. My maternal grandmother opened a beauty parlor in her house. And each day, my mother took the trolley downtown to the dress shop where she worked until the day my father offered her a ride in his Model T Ford. Reportedly, sparks flew.

The bottom line is that I was born in Miami and grew up along the Space Coast, where I live to this day. This makes me one of the few and proud, a native Floridian. It also makes me one very lucky person.

I've stood in my back yard and watched rockets and space shuttles climb until they were only sparkling dots in the sky. I've walked to the beach to watch sea turtles lay their eggs, tears streaming down their sea-worn faces. I've had a drink at Sloppy Joe's and applauded the sunset in Key West. I've snatched sand dollars from the shore and hauled sailfish from the sea. I've scuba dived with sharks (unintentionally, I assure you) and snorkeled with manatee. I have been invaded by pirates in Tampa and attended the World's Largest Outdoor Cocktail Party in Jacksonville. I've sipped Greek coffee in Tarpon Springs and Cuban coffee in Ybor City. I've been to Disney World, Universal Studios, Busch Gardens and my cousin's cattle farm in Hawthorne.

From mammoth theme parks to small farming communities and cow towns, from fishing villages to the greatest space exploration complex in the world, the Sunshine State has something for just about everyone.

Okay, I'll admit that there have been times, while visiting cities like San Francisco and New York that I've considered packing up my sandals and settling down somewhere else. But each time I cross the causeway on my way home and see the regatta of sailboats, houseboats, jet skis and fishing boats on the Indian River and the Atlantic Ocean peeking from the horizon ahead, I'm glad to be here. I've got sand in my shoes and it feels good.

B.J. Bergman-Angstadt

B.J. Bergman-Angstadt is a freelance writer who lives in Indian Harbour Beach. She also teaches literature and writing at Brevard Community College. Exploring the state's nooks and crannies while writing the Florida Weekender column for *Florida Today* newspaper, made her aware of just how delightful and diverse her home state really is.

FABULOUS FLORIDA

1. Florida has more golf courses than any other state.

2. Move over Jaws. A photo proudly posted at the Rod and Reel Pier in Anna Maria shows Frank Cavendish and Dr. Ralph French with their 1973 catch, a 1,386-pound hammerhead shark, measuring 17-feet, one inch.

3. In 1945 Earl Tupper burped and the world has been a safer place for leftovers ever since. Kissimmee is the headquarters of Tupperware Worldwide.

4. Stone crabs are harvested one claw at a time. Claws are taken because they're the best part. Only one is taken so the crab can defend itself while regenerating the missing claw.

5. Florida's baseball greats are honored at the Florida Sports Hall of Fame in Lake City. Among them are Steve Garvey, John "Boog" Powell, Al Rosen, Steve Carlton and George Steinbrenner, who retired to Tampa.

6. Jimmy Buffett was born in Mississippi, a fact Floridians choose to forgive and forget. The state's favorite living adopted son (he'd probably fall right behind Hemingway in an all-time ranking) began his multi-faceted musical and writing career in the Sunshine State. He's also the founder of the Manatee Protection League and initiated the Adopt-a-Manatee program. By the way, when you hear his song, "Margaritaville," the proper response is to stand.

7. According to The International Game Fishing Association, more than 10% of all fly-fishing and saltwater line class world records have been hooked off Key Largo.

8. Want to sleep with the fishes? Jules' Undersea Lodge, the world's only underwater hotel, is located 30 feet down in Key Largo's Emerald Lagoon. The two bedroom digs include a stereo, TV, VCR, microwave, fridge and phone.

9. One of the founders of Anna Maria was John Roser, the inventor of the Fig Newton.

10. Watch out for the vertigo. Lignumvitae boasts the highest spot in the Florida Keys — a dizzying 16 feet above sea level.

11. When he wasn't visiting Captain Tony's Saloon or Sloppy Joe's bar or deep-sea fishing or tending to his flock of six-toed cats, Ernest Hemingway found time in Key West to write *Death in the Afternoon, Green Hills of Africa* and *To Have and Have Not.*

12. Pelican Island became the first National Wildlife Refuge in the country, in 1903 via a proclamation by President Teddy Roosevelt.

13. Missed it by that much. Jules Verne was amazingly on mark when he wrote *From the Earth to the Moon.* His launch site, Bell's Shoals, is less than 100 miles from the actual launch site.

14. During World War II, the Navy developed an elite scuba force, the U.S. Navy Frogmen. The group, known today as Navy Seals, was hatched and hopped into training in Ft. Pierce where nearly 140,000 personnel practiced for D-Day invasion of Europe.

15. Although he was banned from fields in other parts of the state in 1946, Jackie Robinson was welcomed in Daytona. The park where he played is now named Jackie Robinson Ballpark.

16. The state bird, the mockingbird, can get pretty pesky when protecting its young, squawking raucously and dive bombing sleep-dazed residents who attempt to retrieve the morning paper near nests. Still, their popularity can't be disputed. The mockingbird is also the state bird of Arkansas, Mississippi, Tennessee and Texas. Makes you wonder who their P.R. firm is.

17. Florida is the only state where the governor's cabinet consists of six, independently elected state executives.

FABULOUS FLORIDA

18. Here's the dirt. Florida has an official state soil. Myakka soil can be found in more than 1.5 million acres of flat-woods, making it the single most extensive soil in the state.

19. In 1970, 10 months after astronauts blasted off from Kennedy Space Center and landed on the moon, law-makers adopted the moonstone as the official state gem. Moonstone is not native to either Florida or the moon.

20. Just so there's no confusion, residents of Havana in Gadsden County pronounce the name *Hayvana*.

21. Britain traded Havana, Cuba for Florida in 1763 and immediately divided it into two territories — East Florida with a capital at St. Augustine and West Florida with its capital in Pensacola. Both remained loyal to the British during the Revolutionary War. It was probably the last time Floridians agreed on anything.

22. Sorry about that. According to Florida's constitution, the state seal, accepted in 1868, "shall not again be changed after its adoption by the Legislature." While the basic layout — sun's rays, a palm tree, a steamboat on water and an Indian female scattering flowers — has remained, changes in the details just had to be made. It seemed prudent, for instance, to do away with the mountains in the background, since there's not one mountain in the entire state. It also seemed wise to re-clothe the Indian in Seminole garb instead of the original Plains Indian ensemble — including a feathered headdress worn only by males. Other changes include substituting the original cocoa tree with a Sabal palmetto palm, honored as the state tree in 1953.

23. After battling Indians in the First Seminole War, General Andrew Jackson returned to Florida in 1821 to establish a territorial government for the United States and became Florida's first governor.

24. Funny lady Rita Rudner was born in Miami.

FABULOUS FLORIDA

25. The 1957 circus flick *The Greatest Show on Earth* was filmed in Sarasota, then the winter headquarters of Ringling Brothers Circus. The movie, which beat out *High Noon* for the Best Picture Oscar, featured Betty Hutton Charlton Heston and Jimmy Stewart doing most of their own circus stunts.

26. Sea World keeps its Penguin Encounter residents perky with nine tons of man-made snow daily.

27. Don Ameche moon-walked to a Best Supporting Actor Oscar in 1985 with his break-dancing performance in *Cocoon* which was filmed in St. Petersburg.

28. Space vehicles travel at incredible speeds — starting with their trip to the launch pad. A giant crawler moves them from the Vehicle Assembly Building at an unbelievably slow 1 mph.

29. The Spanish introduced the first orange trees to Florida in 1570. Gracias.

30. Defensive back Deacon Jones, born David Jones in Eatonville, introduced the term "sack" to the game of football. It's only fair that he got to name it since he did it so well and so often. One of the L.A. Rams' Fearsome Foursome in the 1960s, Jones was named to the Pro Football Hall of Fame in 1980.

31. Boston pitcher Tim Wakefield hails from Melbourne Beach.

32. One of the world's largest nylon plants is located near Pensacola. Feel like stocking up?

33. Visitors to Miami Beach's Fountainebleu Hotel still request the room where Shirley Eaton met her gilded end in the James Bond movie, *Goldfinger*.

34. Jack Kerouac, the voice of the Beat Generation, spent his last years in St. Petersburg with his mother. The author of *On The Road* and *The Dharma Bums* died on Oct. 20, 1969 at St. Anthony's Hospital there.

35. Falling Waters State Recreation Area contains the state's only waterfall. Okay, so it's really just a ground-level stream making a 100-foot plunge down a wide rock shaft before disappearing into underground cavities; it's still impressive.

36. The Museum of African-American Art in Tampa boasts one of the oldest collections of African-American arts and crafts in the United States.

37. The state saltwater fish is the sailfish, and Stuart is known as the Sailfish Capital of the World.

38. In 1935, Islamorada in the Florida Keys, was devastated by a hurricane believed to be the strongest to ever hit the U.S. The accompanying 17-foot tidal surge claimed about 700 lives, including many World War I veterans who had come to the area to build the Overseas Highway.

39. The state's longest river, the St. Johns (275 miles), is the only major river in the U.S. that flows north.

40. Key West is part of the continental U.S. Yes it is an island. However, just like many other islands along the coast of the U.s., it is located on the continental shelf, making it part of the continent. However, if this still bothers you, you could say the southernmost point in the contiguous United States.

41. The Sunshine State averages 53 inches of rain yearly, mostly accumulated during afternoon downpours lasting only an hour or two. No wonder the unofficial state motto is, "If you don't like the weather, wait a minute."

42. Harriet Beecher Stow, of *Uncle Tom's Cabin* fame, moved to Mandarin with her husband, Calvin, in 1867. The church she founded there was destroyed in a hurricane but has since been rebuilt.

43. A black pirate, called Black Caesar, successfully avoided capture for many years by hiding in the mangroves of Biscayne Bay. Finally, however, he was found and hung.

44. Baby alert. Corkscrew Swamp is home to the largest colony of wood storks in the nation.

FABULOUS FLORIDA

45. Sanibel Island may be the only place in the world with an official posture. "The Sanibel Stoop" is the position taken to retrieve samples of the more than 200 varieties of shells found there.

46. Early rockets launched from Cape Canaveral were nicknamed "snake chasers" because, more often than not, they lurched onto their sides upon lift-off and zoomed through the palmetto-filled wilderness surrounding the launch pad.

47. Thanks to billboards across the nation, Ron Jon Surf Shop in Cocoa Beach has grown from a hole-in-the-wall surfboard and baggies store to a garish, neon-colored, complex, with an indoor waterfall and parking lot attendants. A favorite destination of Space Coast insomniacs, Ron Jon's is open 24 hours a day, 365 days a year.

48. Go jump in a lake? In Orlando, that's easy to do with more than 50 lakes within the city limits.

49. The favorite tourist attraction in Key West is the sunset. Each evening, visitors and locals alike head for Mallory Square to applaud the setting sun.

50. John D. Rockefeller died at his Ormond Beach winter home, the Casements, in 1937.

51. Lionel Barrymore, Oliver Hardy and the Keystone Kops all began their careers in Jacksonville, the first motion picture capital. Major studios, weary of northern winters, moved production to the area between 1910 and 1920. But residents, protesting wild car chases through city streets and the movies' often sexual themes, chased the industry to Hollywood, Calif. This fact makes the Florida Film Commission cringe.

52. The sky's the limit for Orlando's Joe Kittinger. In 1960, he became the first person to parachute from 102,000 feet. In 1984, he broke another record by becoming the first to fly a balloon solo across the Atlantic.

53. The world's only fully-rigged pirate ship and its crew of 700 rowdy buccaneers invade Tampa each February during the Gasparilla Pirate Fest. The city's surrender is always swift. Then the Pirates, joined by loyal locals, parade in victory down Bayshore Boulevard, tossing treasure to the crowds as they pass. Ahoy, matey.

54. In the pits? You can be at Daytona USA, a 50,000-square-foot interactive motor-racing museum complex. One of its most popular attractions is a simulated pit stop where visitors try to beat the clock by changing four tires on a race car in under 20 seconds.

55. Hurricane Andrew, which hit the Homestead area in 1992, was the costliest natural disaster in United States history, causing more than $20 billion in damage. The storm killed 38 people and left 250,000 homeless.

56. Florida mines about 85 percent of the nation's phosphate rock which is used in fertilizer and livestock feed. My, look at those cows grow!

57. Jennifer Capriati's family moved to Lauderhill when she was four years old so she could learn to serve and smash from Jimmy Evert, father of tennis powerhouse, Chris Evert. Just shy of her 14th birthday, Capriati became the youngest American and second-youngest tennis player ever to turn pro.

58. Think Key West is part of the United States? Don't you believe it. On April 23, 1982, Key West Mayor Dennis Wardlow officially seceded from the Union, established the Conch Republic, declared war, surrendered and demanded foreign aid. The U.S. government has never responded to Wardlow's notification, which locals (who call themselves as Conchs) view as acceptance of their terms.

59. No doubt, Florida State football has been hot in the 1990s. The Seminoles have won all but one bowl game (its only loss was to University of Florida in the 1997 Sugar Bowl) and 96.7% of their games against out-of-state opponents in regular season.

60. Florida shares with Georgia the country's largest deposits of fuller's earth, the main ingredient in cat litter. Here kitty, kitty.

61. The Bogart-Bacall classic, *Key Largo,* wasn't filmed in the city by the same name. Truth is, the town on the Florida Key's northernmost island was known as Rock Harbor before the movie's 1952 release. City fathers re-dubbed the place hoping to cash in on the film's publicity and popularity. It's a case of life imitating art for fun and profit.

62. His name really was Mudd. When Dr. Samuel Mudd set a leg for John Wilkes Booth, he had no idea he was aiding Abraham Lincoln's assassin. Nonetheless, he was sentenced to life at hard labor and sent to Ft. Jefferson on the Tortugas, a remote chain of rock islands west of Key West. His valiant efforts to save inmates during a Yellow Fever epidemic earned a pardon from President Andrew Johnson on the last day of his presidency.

FABULOUS FLORIDA

63. In 1905, Greek divers started sponge-fishing at Tarpon Springs and the area became the nation's most important sponge producer. Today, man-made sponge manufacturers have soaked up that honor.

64. Lake Okeechobee, 35 miles long and 25 miles wide, is Florida's largest lake and the fourth largest natural lake within the United States. Not surprisingly, Okeechobee is the Indian word for "big water."

65. Florida is a really swinging place. Daytona Beach is headquarters of the LPGA. Ponte Vedra is home to PGA Tour. And PGA America, where pros train, is located in Palm Beach Gardens.

66. Perry calls itself the Eclipse Capital of the World but don't expect to see a solar light show if you visit there. The town adopted the name after 40,000 scientists and amateur sun-spotters from across the globe gathered there on March 7, 1970 to get the best view the solar eclipse that day.

FABULOUS FLORIDA

67. Tom Petty and his Heartbreakers hail from Gainesville, where they played local clubs before "Free Fallin' " to L.A.

68. The residents of Key West have a time-honored custom for dealing with the limited space in their cemetery. When a family plot is full, the bones of the long deceased are dug up and put in a small wooden box, which is often placed in the casket with the newly departed. Talk about your strange bedfellows.

69. More college football bowl games are played in Florida than in any other state. Pass the turkey.

70. "To all the teams I've loved before. I love the Miami Heat more." Well, Julio Inglesias might have sung that. After all, he's part-owner of the basketball team.

71. To correctly pronounce Kissimmee, assuming you're looking for the city and not a little romance, put the emphasis on the second syllable.

72. If you build it, they will come. That's what Clyde Perky thought when he constructed a 35-foot bat tower on Sugarloaf Key. He filled it with bat dung he'd shipped over from Texas. Then, he waited for the bats to check in and dine on the swarms of mosquitoes that bombarded guests to his restaurant and cottages. He waited some more. They never showed. Eventually, modern techniques solved the mosquito problem. The tower still stands as a tribute to a batty idea.

73. Pensacola-born Daniel "Chappie" James, Jr., one of the famed Tuskegee Airmen, served as a combat pilot in World War II and Korea before becoming the first black four-star general and head of NORAD in 1975.

74. Since 1947, the world's only captive mermaids have lived at Weeki Wachee Springs, entertaining guests by eating, drinking and breathing underwater. Okay, they're really women in costumes, and they breathe through a tube. But you try to eat a banana underwater.

75. Apopka is the Indoor Foliage Capital of the World, even though it's named after an outdoor plant. Apopka means "large potato."

76. The Gulf Stream is actually an ocean-going river. It wiggles in close to Florida on its sea trek through the Atlantic from the Gulf of Mexico to Europe.

77. Bascom-born Faye Dunaway has been nominated for three Academy Awards, winning the 1976 Best Actress Oscar for her role in *Network*.

78. No place in Florida is more than 60 miles from open water. Did you say something about the humidity?

79. Back in the 1950s, Daytona car racing meant a spin in the sand. The original course included a long stretch down the World's Most Famous Beach. Those early races inspired Daytona's Bill France, Sr. to form NASCAR — now the world's largest race organization and build the Daytona International Speedway.

80. Rotten veggies and water balloons fly each April during a mock sea battle at Key West. The naval nuttery is part of the annual Conch Republic Independence Celebration, commemorating Key West's 1982 secession from the United States. Smack in the middle of the 10-day event, thoughtful islanders have set aside one day for hangover recovery.

81. Each Spring and Fall, Florida is invaded by swarms of kamikaze insects that smash into cars on the state's highways, coating windshields and threatening paint jobs. They're called love bugs, although no one, with the exception of car wash owners, even likes them. Their name comes from the fact that they're always seen in pairs — mating in mid-air. No one seems to know for sure where they came from. The theory that they were experimented on and released by the University of Florida was pooh-poohed by U of F entomologist Jim Lloyd. "If we had invented them," he was quoted as saying in the *Orlando Sentinel*, "they'd be bigger and could carry people off."

FABULOUS FLORIDA

82. Florida has 1,250 miles of coastline, more than any other state except Alaska.

83. Physicist Theodore Maiman created the first laser at Hughes Research Laboratories in Miami in 1960. What a bright idea.

84. The Florida Museum of Natural History in Gainesville is the South's largest natural history museum and is considered one of the top ten in the nation.

85. He might have Georgia on his mind — why not, he was born there — but Ray Charles was raised in Greenville. When he lost his sight to glaucoma, at age 7, he enrolled at the St. Augustine School for Deaf and Blind Children where his love of music was nurtured and his talents honed. The 12-time Grammy winner received an honorary doctorate of Fine Arts from the University of South Florida in 1990.

86. Name that group. Jacksonville native Ronnie Van Zant — lead singer of the rock group Lynyrd Skynyrd — was instrumental in naming the band. His inspiration was a physical education teacher, Leonard Skinner.

87. Arnie's Army still gathers when Arnold Palmer plays in Bay Hill where he lives.

88. The new Jerusalem is located just south of Fort Meyers, at least according to Dr. Cyrus Teed, a Chicago physician who founded the Koreshan Unity commune there in 1894. Teed taught that the universe is a giant, hollow ball in which the Earth and other heavenly bodies resided. Teed also claimed to be immortal but died in 1908 at the age of 69. His followers donated the land to the state. It is now the Koreshan State Park.

89. Florida has more jai alai frontons than anyplace else in the world, and Miami's 5,100-seat arena is the world's largest. By the way, it's pronounced *High-Lie*.

FABULOUS FLORIDA

90. One of the highlights of St. Augustine's annual weeklong Easter celebration is the Parade de los Caballos y Conches — a traditional Easter parade with a twist. Joining the human celebrants are horses in their Easter bonnets, hats donated by celebrities such as Marilyn Quayle and Loni Anderson.

91. Babe Ruth was a regular visitor to New York Yankee spring training games in St. Petersburg after retiring to Florida in 1935. In the 1940s, the Bambino passed along his diamond savvy at Ray Doan's Baseball School in Palatka.

92. Before illusionist Harry Houdini died, he left his wife, Beatrice, a copy of a message he promised to send from beyond the grave. Titusville clairvoyant, Arthur A. Ford, brought Houdini's widow the correct message — "Rosabelle, believe."

93. Key West is only 92 nautical miles from Cuba. It is 177 miles from Miami.

94. The best way to traverse the Everglades is by airboat, but you can do it by car. Try the Everglades Parkway, better known as Alligator Alley, or US 41, called the Tamiami Trail.

95. Julia Tuttle, the "Mother of Miami," had visions for the South Florida wilderness that weren't apparent to Henry Flagler. His railroad originally ended at Palm Beach where he had built an estate. In 1895, when a freeze wiped out most of the state's citrus crop, Tuttle sent Flagler an orange blossom and offered him part of her land if he would extend his railroad and help her lay out the town of Miami. It was an offer he couldn't refuse.

96. While playing for the Orlando Magic, Shaquille O'Neal became the first rookie in pro basketball history ever to be named Player of the Week after only one week in the game.

97. Remember Spanish I? Then you know that the name of classy Boca Raton means "rat's mouth."

98. They call him Mr. Poitier. The barrier-busting career of Miami-born Sidney Poitier has been filled with firsts. He was the first black actor nominated for a Best Actor Oscar and the first to win one. He was also the first black actor to play a romantic lead and to be named the nation's top box office draw. By the way, he also directed 1980's top box office smash, *Stir Crazy*.

99. Believe it or not, Ripley dubbed Key West's main drag, Duval Street, "The world's longest street." Although it is only a little more than a mile long, it does reach from the Atlantic Ocean to the Gulf of Mexico.

100. Camp Blanding Military Training Center near Stark trained a total of 1 million soldiers during World War II. Today it is home to a WW II museum and Florida's National Guard.

101. Florida is the top producer of oranges and grapefruit in the U.S., growing about three-fourths of the annual crop. How sweet, and sour, it is.

102. March is a month of celebration in Miami's Little Havana section. The fun starts with a 23-block street party called Calle Ocho, where the Guiness record for the longest conga line (119,986 dancers) was set in 1988. Wrapping up the festivities is a week-long Rio-style carnival, it is the nation's largest Hispanic celebration.

103. The waters off the Florida Keys boast the only living coral reef in the continental United States.

104. The *African Queen* is still a spunky boat. The nautical star of the picture by the same name has carried its current owner, Jim Hendricks, across the English Channel and regularly takes tourists for boat tours around Key Largo. When Hendricks isn't toting the *Queen* to classic film festivals around the country, she resides at Key Largo's Holiday Inn docks.

105. Entertainer Jackie Gleason dubbed his adopted home, Miami Beach, The Sun and Fun Capital of the World.

FABULOUS FLORIDA

106. Hall of Famer Pete Pihos, who was born in Miami, spent his entire football career playing tight end for the Philadelphia Eagles. He was named All-Pro six times.

107. To University of Florida fans it's known simply as, "The Kick." The year was 1966. The opponent was Auburn. The game was about to end and the score was tied at 27. With fourth down and forever to go, Steve Spurrier — the quarterback — kicked a 40-yard field goal that won the game and cinched Spurrier's Heisman Trophy, the state's first. Exactly 30 years later, the University had its second Heisman winner, Danny Wuerffel. His head coach: Steve Spurrier.

108. Jackie Gleason is buried at Our Lady of Mercy Cemetery in Miami. His tombstone is appropriately engraved, "And Away We Go."

109. Paula Hawkins of Winter Park was elected Florida's first female Senator in 1980.

110. Between 1980 and 1990, Florida's population increased by 32.7%.

111. For more than 100 years, visitors eager to peek into the future or contact loved ones "on the other side" have headed for Cassadaga, founded by a trance medium named George Colby in 1894 as a place where Spiritualists could live and work together. The Southern Cassadaga Spiritualist Camp Meeting Association is the oldest active religious community in the Southeastern United States. And you thought mediums were rare.

112. No doubt about it, the sands of Fort Walton Beach are among the most dazzling white in the world. According to rumor, unsavory types sold it as sugar during World War II.

113. The Reverend Billy Graham graduated from Florida Bible College in Temple Terrace and began his preaching career on a Tampa sidewalk.

FABULOUS FLORIDA

114. Going in circles, big time. With world-class race sites such as the Daytona International Speedway, Sebring Raceway, the Homestead Motorsports Complex and the new Disney World racetrack, more major motorsports events are held in Florida than in any other state.

115. Talented Miami-born entertainer Ben Vereen earned an Emmy nomination for his portrayal of Chicken George in *Roots* and a Best Actor Tony Award for his work in the Broadway musical *Pippin*.

116. For more than 50 years, Redland Fruit and Spice Park in Dade County has been known to grow and sell the best and most extensive selection of tropical fruits and vegetables to be found anywhere. For the particularly picky, they carry 50 varieties of bananas.

117. If you've always dreamed of swimming with dolphins, head for the Florida Keys where two facilities can make your dream come true: Theater of the Sea on Islamorada, and Dolphins Plus on Grassy Key.

118. One small step for Harry Truman, one giant leap . . . . in 1949 President Truman signed a law making Cape Canaveral the official testing site for guided missile development and assigned nearby Patrick Air Force Base (formerly the Banana River Naval Air Station) to supply support to the fledgling space program.

119. The Indian River isn't a river at all. It's a lagoon, separated from the Atlantic Ocean by 155 miles of barrier island. With more than 4,000 plant and animal species — 36 of them rare or endangered — the Indian River Lagoon is North America's most diverse estuary.

120. Romanian Olympic superstar Nadia Comaneci defected to South Florida in 1989.

121. Francisco Gordillo, who once sailed with Columbus, is credited with naming Cape Canaveral. He came up with the name, which means place of the cane bearers, after Indians using cane arrows attacked him and his men.

122. Burt Reynolds' roommate and football teammate at Florida State University was future ESPN college football analyst Lee Corso.

123. Oh Lucy! Desi Arnez attended St. Patrick's Catholic School in Miami Beach.

124. A memorial to Confederate Secretary of State Judah P. Benjamin stands in Ellenton on the grounds of the Gamble Plantation, the only antebellum plantation house surviving in South Florida. Benjamin hid from Union soldiers there at the end of the Civil War.

125. No pictures were ever made of the stained glass interior of Tallahassee's old capitol building dome but that didn't stop restoration efforts. Guided by 100 pounds of broken glass found in a storeroom, workers were able to recreate the design.

126. Football commentator and former football star Chris Collinsworth hails from Titusville.

127. Fly me to the moon. The first men on the moon — Neil Armstrong and Edwin Aldrin — were launched from Cape Kennedy on July 16, 1969. Michael Collins also made the historic flight but stayed on board the orbiting command module.

128. The Fantasy of Flight Museum in Polk City boasts the world's largest private collection of vintage airplanes. The museum also includes four flight simulators where visitors can experience air raids over WWI's Western Front and WWII's South Pacific.

129. The oldest continuously inhabited town in North America, St. Augustine, was founded in 1565 — that's 42 years before Jamestown and 55 years before the Pilgrims landed.

130. *Columbia*, the first reusable spacecraft — AKA space shuttle — was launched from Kennedy Space Center on April 12, 1981 carrying astronauts John Young and Robert Crippen.

131. With a successful re-election bid in 1988, 88-year-old Claude Pepper of Coral Gables became the oldest person ever elected to Congress. Pepper was one of the authors of Franklin Roosevelt's New Deal and spent his last years fighting for the rights of senior citizens.

132. Worth Avenue in Palm Beach has been dubbed Rodeo Drive East.

133. About 50,000 people a year tour Florida's capitol building in Tallahassee, one of only four skyscraper state capitols in the nation. The others are in Baton Rouge, La.; Lincoln, Neb.; and Bismarck, N.D.

134. Astronaut Alan B. Shepard, Jr. became the first American in space when Friendship 7 was launched from Cape Canaveral on May 5, 1961.

135. George Hamilton started on that great tan in Palm Beach where he graduated from Palm Beach High.

136. After moving to Apalachicola in 1840, Dr. John Gorrie tinkered to find a way to cool sickrooms and make his patients more comfortable. The result? A machine that made ice. Today, a statue of Gorrie stands in Washington D.C., honoring him as the Father of Air Conditioning and Refrigeration. What a cool guy.

137. Pam Godwin and her husband, Guy Manos of Key Largo have made a career of dropping in on people, from very high up, wearing parachutes. Together and separately, the couple has provided skydiving stunts for dozens of television shows, commercials and movies — including the Wesley Snipes movie *Drop Zone*, Manos's first screenplay.

138. Sculptor Augusta Christine Savage, born in Green Cove Springs in 1892, became the first African-American to be accepted into the National Association of Women Painters and Sculptors in 1934.

139. The chandelier that lit Twelve Oaks plantation in the movie *Gone with the Wind* now shines at the Sarasota Opera House. Fiddle-dee-dee.

140. The Izaak Walton Fishing Club, founded on Useppa Island in 1912 by publisher Barron Collier, claims to be the birthplace of catch-and-release fishing. The only thing members were allowed to keep from the tarpon they caught was a single scale on which they wrote their names and the weight of the catch.

141. Sherman Field in Pensacola is home to the Navy's famous precision flying team, the Blue Angels.

142. How much does it cost to rent an island? Ask the CIA. They rented Useppa Island — once vacation get-a-way for Rockefellers, Du Ponts, Teddy Roosevelt and Mae West — as a training site for Cuban radio operators preparing for the Bay of Pigs invasion.

143. Jensen Beach is the Sea Turtle Capital of the World.

144. Maps as early as 1563 show Cape Canaveral, making it one of the oldest landmarks in North America. No wonder residents raised a ruckus when President Lyndon Johnson renamed the place Cape Kennedy just weeks after John Kennedy's assassination in 1963. With 400 years of history on their side, locals finally won a 10-year battle to restore the original name. Well, it seemed like a good idea at the time.

145. St. Augustine gets the glory but Ft. Caroline, just up the coast near present-day Jacksonville, deserves the honors as the first European settlement in the New World. In fact, one of the reasons the Spanish founded St. Augustine, a year after French Huguenots and soldiers arrived at Ft. Caroline, was to eradicate the French settlement. Which they did.

146. The Florida Everglades cover all or parts of seven counties — Glade, Hendry, Martin, Palm Beach, Broward, Dade and Monroe.

FABULOUS FLORIDA

147. One of the largest cigar factories in the world was built in Tampa by Martinez Ybor in 1886. To make the long workdays go faster, his employees chipped in to hire *lectores*, who read newspapers and books to them as they worked.

148. Tallahassee was the only Confederate capitol East of the Mississippi not captured by the Union in the Civil War.

149. The Conch House Restaurant in St. Augustine is owned and operated by the Ponces, descendants of the Solanas, probably the oldest family in the United States. Family records, kept at the city's Catholic cathedral, are documented all the way back to 1594.

150. Forestry is Florida's third largest industry, and Perry is the Tree Capital of the South. The city celebrates each October by crowning a Forestry Queen, holding chainsaw championships and serving the World's Largest Free-Feathered Fish (chicken) Fry.

151. Stock car racer Bobby Allison was born in Miami in 1937.

152. Play ball! Florida is the Spring Training Capital of the World. All but five of today's major league baseball teams have gotten into the swing in Florida towns.

153. The largest bald cypress tree in the U.S. is located along the General Hutchinson Parkway between Sanford and Longwood. Known as The Senator, the tree is 126 feet high, 17 fi feet in diameter and estimated to be more than 3,000 years old.

154. Early settler Ralph Middleton Munroe founded Coconut Grove and built his one-story home, the Barnacle, there. When his growing family demanded more room, Munroe simply jacked up the entire structure and built a new first floor.

155. The Loxahatchee River holds the distinction of being the only National Wild and Scenic River in Florida.

156. The International Worm Fiddling competition takes place in Caryville during Labor Day weekend. You won't see worms with tiny Stradivariuses or fiddles with earthworm strings. "There's not no music," says organizer Joanne Palmer. Worm fiddling is a time-honored practice for getting bait. A two-by-four is pounded into the ground and an ax is rubbed back and forth across the board's rough top edge, producing vibrations that lure worms to the surface.

157. The Asolo Theater was built in 1798 but not in Sarasota where it now stands. It was shipped from Venice, Italy, but it wasn't built there either. It was relocated to Venice — where it sat in storage for 20 years — from its original site in Scotland. Asolo made its Sarasota debut in 1958 and today is one of Florida's four official state theaters.

158. St. Augustine's Café Alcazar is probably the only café in the world located in a pool. The pool is drained, so be careful when you dive into your food.

159. Grab your hog. Motorcycles have zoomed to Daytona Beach for Bike Week since 1937.

160. It's not the Alps but apparently the 10-foot high rock playground Jim Berke built for his goats is good enough. Each year his Turtle Creek Dairy in Loxahatchee produces about 20,000 pounds of the state's only authentic, European-style, gourmet goat cheeses. Such far-from-cheesy notables as Prince Charles, George Bush, Donald Trump, Queen Elizabeth and Oprah Winfrey have enjoyed his novel nanny knoshes.

161. Miami Vice blasted onto television screens in 1984, and suddenly no socks and a two-day beard growth were hip. The show, which was shot in Miami and featured Miami Beach's Art Deco District, ran until 1989.

162. Miami boasts the only four-time Cy Young Award winner. Pitcher Steve Carlton was born there in 1944.

163. The New World's first known Christmas celebration was held in Florida by Hernando de Soto and his men in 1539.

164. At the opening of the 1997 football season, Miami Dolphin quarterback Dan Marino was the all-time leader in touchdown pass attempts, completions and yardage.

165. John F. Kennedy wrote the 1956 Pulitzer Prize-winner, *Profiles in Courage,* at the Kennedy estate in Palm Beach.

166. *Good Times* actress Esther Rolle was born in Pompano Beach in 1933.

167. Most places don't brag about their trash heaps but the people of Osprey put theirs on display. Osprey is the only place in the United States where you can actually enter an ancient Indian shell midden (the archeological term for trash heap) and see bones and garbage of a by gone civilization.

168. Florida State is one of only two college football teams in the nation to finish each of the last six seasons ranked in the Top 10 in the final AP Poll. The other team — the University of Florida.

169. In 1953, after 15 months at sea, Ann Davison landed at Miami to become the first woman to sail solo across the Atlantic.

170. Additions have been made to the Walton-DeFuniak Public Library since it opened in a 24-by-17 foot room in 1887 but it remains the state's oldest public library operating in its original building. Besides 30,000 volumes, some as old as the library itself, it houses a fine European armor collection.

171. The Ocala National Forest is the southernmost national forest in the continental U.S.

172. Cocoa Beach is the East Coast Surfing Capital. Come on over and hang 10. Heck, hang 20 if you'd like.

FABULOUS FLORIDA

173. About 10,000 U.S. soldiers and sailors poured into Key West as the Spanish-American War loomed. They came with a great thirst — about 100,000 gallons of fresh water and an untold amount of liquor was shipped in — and remarkably bad manners. At one point, Rough Riders trotted their horses into a Key West Cuban-cuisine restaurant. The incident became known as the Charge of the Yellow Rice Brigade.

174. In 1991, Palm Bay's Kim Adler, a striking woman, was named Rookie of the Year by the Ladies Pro-Bowling Tour. She was runner-up for Player of the Year in 1996.

175. New Smyrna is known as The World's Safest Beach because offshore reefs protect its coast from killer riptides.

176. The water sport of couch potatoes, that's tubing down the Ichetucknee River. About 3,000 people a day join the regatta of tubes, rafts — in fact, anything that floats — on a leisurely 1-mph river ride.

177. Before retiring to Winter Haven, Betty Skelton Frank was known worldwide as a fast woman. In 1933, she became the first female inductee of the International Automotive Hall of Fame after breaking the world's land speed record for women four times and topping 300 mph at the Bonneville Salt Flats. She was also the first woman elected to the Aerobatic Hall of Fame in 1988. Her plane, *The Little Stinker*, is on display at the Nnational Air and Space Museum in Washington, D.C.

178. Eight different flags — French, Spanish, British American Patriots, Green Cross of Florida, Mexican, Confederate and United States — have flown over Amelia Island — the only place in the United States with that distinction.

179. Shipwrecks were once so frequent in Florida waters that in 1888, the federal government built five houses of refuge along the coast where wreck survivors could rest and recuperate. One of these houses still stands in Stuart.

FABULOUS FLORIDA

180. Since 1983, Florida colleges have picked up six National Football Championships. The University of Miami leads with four National Titles. Florida State and University of Florida have one each.

181. America's smallest post office measures a tad more than 8 feet by 7 feet and is located in Ochopee.

182. Daytona Beach is 500 feet wide at low tide, providing plenty of sunning and parking spots on the hard-packed sand.

183. Escambia and St. Johns were the first two counties in the state. Both were established on July 21, 1821.

184. St. Petersburg is the home of the Major League Baseball Players Alumni Association and the site of the nation's longest established old-timers game.

185. Vowel-uptuous Vanna White was born in Miami in 1957.

186. Wendys guy Dave Thomas graduated from Coconut Creek High School on March 25, 1993, 45 years after dropping out. It was a biggie day.

187. Amelia Island is one of the last places along the Atlantic where you can ride horseback on the beach. Giddy-up.

188. The nation's first offshore shrimp trawlers sailed from the docks of Fernandina Beach, the only town in the country that has a shrimp net manufacturer on site to accommodate the fleet.

189. With a wealth of offbeat epitaphs, such as "I told you I was sick" and "Harry, I know where you are sleeping tonight," the Key West Cemetery one of the most popular attractions on the island.

190. Gainesville was named after General Edmund Gaines who captured Aaron Burr and led U.S. troops during Florida's Second Seminole War.

191. The world's smallest police station is located in Carrabelle. When not patrolling the tiny burg, home to about 1,500 people and outlying areas, the city's four police officers can be found parked outside the station — a public phone booth decorated with a painting of an American Flag — waiting for the next exciting call.

192. In 1967, Betty Mae Tiger Jumper — who was born in Indiantown to a white father and Seminole mother — became the Seminole's first female tribal chairman. After graduating from high school, one of the first Florida Seminoles to do so, she went on to become a nurse and is credited with bringing modern health care to her people.

193. The 16-foot thick walls of the Castillo de San Marcos in St. Augustine are made of native coquina rock which is composed of shells. The Castillo, a replacement for a wooden fort razed by Sir Francis Drake in 1586, took 24 years to build.

194. Detective Travis McGee might be just a character in a book but his book-bound home, Berth f18 at Bahia Mar, really exists. The people of Fort Lauderdale set up the berth, designated with a special marker, to honor McGee's creator, John D. MacDonald, who lived in Siesta Key.

195. The largest street rod show in the Southeast takes place each October at Tampa's Florida State Fair-Grounds.

196. Lion Country Safari in West Palm Beach is a zoo in reverse. Scores of African species roam freely while visitors are caged in their cars. This novel attraction was the first cageless zoo in the nation.

197. According to the 1990 census, more than 30,000 million-aires call Florida home. Nice neighborhood.

198. The world's largest key lime pie, more than 15-feet in diameter, was created in Captiva in 1987.

FABULOUS FLORIDA

199. You can see the original manuscript of the book, *The Black Stallion* in the Farley Children's Wing of the Venice Public Library. Author Walter Farley's Smith-Corona typewriter and his riding gear also are on display.

200. Forget trick or treat. In Ybor City, residents celebrate Guavaween. The Latin-style festivities kick off with a parade called the Mama Guava Stumble.

201. Eatonville is the oldest black municipality in the U.S. Incorporated in 1887, the town billed itself as a Negro city governed by Negroes.

202. The 1963 movie, *Flipper,* shot in Miami, was written by *the Creature from the Black Lagoon.* Kinda. Screenwriter Ricou Browning played the Creature in that 1954 flick which was filmed at Wakulla Springs.

203. The world's largest doors (four of them measuring 460-feet high) are found at the Vehicle Assembly Building at Kennedy Space Center.

204. The Ormond garage was built in 1903 to prepare and service many of the pioneer autos that raced on Ormond Beach. Among the famous drivers who set world speed records there were William K. Vanderbilt, Jr., Fred Marriott and Barney Oldfield.

205. Janet Reno, the first woman attorney general of the United States, was born in Miami in 1938.

206. It meant finishing ahead of schedule but Fort Lauderdale's first tourist hotel, the Broward, was completed in time to house the cast and crew filming the 1918 movie, *The Idol Dancer*. The first name on the register is that of producer D.W. Griffith.

207. Florida's highest point, 345 feet above sea level, is lower than the lowest elevation in 16 states.

208. David Levy, Florida's first senator and the first Jew in the nation to hold that post, later changed his name to Yulee.

209. It isn't in the *Lethal Weapon 3* credits but the part of the International Control Systems Building — you remember, the one that blew to smithereens in the film's first five minutes — was played, most convincingly, by Orlando's old City Hall. Seems when the flick's producers found out about plans implode the building, they wrote it into a new opening scene and flew cast and crew in for the event. Former Orlando Mayor Bill Frederick also was cast, in a less demanding role, as head of the bomb squad.

210. Locals have gotten so familiar with a sinkhole that keeps gobbling up a section of I-75, they're on a first-name basis. They've christened it Mikey, after the kid in the Life cereal commercial. Yum asphalt. Mikey likes it.

211. Stetson University wasn't really named for a hat. It was named for the creator of the hat, John Batterson Stetson, whose large donations to Deland Academy prompted its renaming in 1889.

212. In Florida it will rain on one side of the street but not the other. It can also rain while the sun is shining.

213. Porch lights are disorienting, so Lights Out For Turtles signs pop up along Atlantic beaches from May to September when giant sea turtles make the arduous night-time journey from the sea to soft sand along the dunes to lay their eggs.

214. From scuba divers dressed as mermaids to white jumpsuit-clad Snorkeling Elvises, the crowds at the Annual Lower Keys Underwater Music Festival are as entertaining as the tunes. The six-hour broadcast makes its way down into the waters of Looe Key National Marine Sanctuary via special speakers attached to the bottoms of boats spaced along the reef.

215. Want to see something scary? Drive to the bottom of Spook Hill in Lake Wales, throw the transmission in neutral, shut off the engine and wait. The car will travel back up the hill for about 100 feet.

216. It took 1,000 artisans more than five years to create Villa Viscaya, the Miami winter home of farm machinery magnate James Deering. The authentic Italian palazzo was completed in 1916, at a cost of more than $15 million. Additional millions were spent to procure the fabulous collection of European art treasures inside. Deering purchased (and replaced) the roofs of entire Cuban villages to get enough weathered, handmade tiles to roof his new home.

217. Cayo Hueso, the name Spanish explorers gave Key West, means Isle of Bones. Although no one knows for sure, the bones they found littering the island might have belonged to Calusa and Carib Indians who battled over fishing spots.

218. Like most beachfront dwellers, Molly Wilmot was used to finding flotsam in her backyard after a storm. But when a 230-foot Venezuelan tanker, *Mercedes* I, beached behind her sea wall in 1984, she was not happy. It took for 103 days to free the vessel.

219. The oldest building in the Western Hemisphere is located on North Miami Beach. The Cloisters of the Monastery of St. Bernard, built in Spain in 1141 A.D., was purchased in 1925 by publisher William Randolph Hearst, who had it shipped over in 10,751 boxes. When customs agents refused to open the boxes, fearing that the packing straw might be contaminated, Hearst lost interest. The monastery was finally reassembled three years after Hearst died.

220. Rubber Nose Capital? The first clown college in the U.S. opened in 1958 in St. Petersburg.

221. A 100-foot dragon named Hope stands on the southern-most point of Merritt Island, where the Banana and Indian Rivers meet. The concrete creature was constructed in 1971, based on an Indian legend of dragons that guarded the area. On special occasions, a pot of fire is inserted through a trap door to make the dragon's eyes glow.

222. On Jan. 19, 1977, it snowed in Miami.

223. In 1969, Diane Crump became the first female jockey to ride at Hialiah Race Park.

224. Pensacola native Jacqueline Cochran grabbed more speed, distance and altitude records than any other pilot of her time. Raised in foster homes and forced to leave school after the third grade to work in a cotton mill, she went on to earn her pilot's license after only three weeks of training. During World War II, she organized and led the Women's Air Force Service Pilots (WASP). In 1964, she flew at more than twice the speed of sound. Cochran was inducted into the Aviation Hall of Fame in 1971.

225. Ducks are making a big splash in Key West. The World War II remnant amphibious vessels — which go from bus to boat at the flip of a switch — are the newest way to tour the island.

226. Each year, tourists pour more than $26 billion into Florida's economy. Thank you very much.

227. Cassius Clay, later known as Muhammad Ali, made his big-time boxing debut in Miami Beach on Feb. 25, 1964, beating heavy weight champ Sonny Liston in a technical knockout.

228. Many a diver feels compelled to touch the Christ of the Deep, a 9-foot statue located 20-feet under the water at Key Largo Dry Rocks. But be warned, stinging fire coral has made the statue its home. Holy hot-stuff.

229. Although we're sure it had nothing to do with the service there, the rock classic (*I Can't Get No*) *Satisfaction* was written by the Rolling Stones as they sat by the pool of the Clearwater Hotel.

230. St. Petersburg-born Terrence McNally turned to play writing after touring the world with John Steinbeck's family as the children's tutor. His Obie-winning *Bad Habits* was the first play ever to make the leap from Off-Broadway to Broadway. Bravo!

231. A large, white Air Force blimp, called *Fat Albert,* used to be a familiar sight cruising along Florida's East Coast, looking for drug-smuggling boats. Today, it has a permanent home, attached to a 10,000-foot cable above Cudjoe Key.

232. The Salvador Dali Museum in St. Petersburg is packed with the largest and most comprehensive collection of the surrealist's works in the world. More 300 paintings, 1,000 graphics and an eclectic assortment of sculptures and *objets d' art* are housed in a beautiful building by the bay.

233. Heated debate over moving Florida's capital from Tallahassee to more centrally-located Orlando was stopped cold in 1970 when North Florida legislators finagled approval to build a new skyscraper capitol building. Their idea was to construct a building so expensive that it would be cost prohibitive to ever relocate the state's political headquarters. Your tax dollars at work.

234. Rowdy Gaines may be all wet, but he's The Pride of Winter Haven. Gaines won three Gold medals in swimming at the 1984 Olympics in Los Angeles and presently holds several Masters long course freestyle records in the 30-34 age group.

235. Local television stations covered the birth when Baby Shamu became the first killer whale born in captivity, on Sept. 26, 1985 at Orlando's Sea World.

236. Florida football teams have had their share of legal problems but none compare to the 1912 University of Florida Gators who skipped the country to avoid prosecution. The country they fled was Cuba. The Gators had been invited to play two games against Cuban all-star teams. They won the first without incident but ran into problems during the second, five days later. When Coach G.E. Pyle finally refused to play because of creative rule interpretations by the referee, fans spilled from the stands, a riot ensued and Pyle spent the night in jail. When he was released to await trial, he gathered up his players and sneaked back to the States.

237. Florida's first television station was WTVJ-TV in Miami.

238. The Florida's Panhandle has been unofficially dubbed the Redneck Riviera. If you mention this fact to a local, be sure to smile.

239. The oldest water ski show in the nation continues today at Cypress Gardens in Winter Haven.

240. The Orlando Tourist Commission can't help but be pleased that the city is now in Orange County — originally named Mosquito County.

241. South Florida's first black settlers hailed from the Bahamas, a fact that is celebrated annually at Miami's Goombay Festival, the largest African-American heritage celebration in the country.

242. An omen? The Tampa Bay Buccaneers lost their first 26 games in a row.

243. Although the rest of the state sets its clocks by Eastern Standard Time, the bulk of the Panhandle West of the Apalachicola River is in the Central Time Zone.

244. Pensacola National Museum of Naval Aviation, the world's only museum of its type, is located on the grounds of the world's largest naval air station. Exhibits include a replica of the first Navy aircraft, circa 1911 and the Skylab command module.

245. The city of Jacksonville is one of the largest in the country. In 1968, the city limits were expanded to include all of Duval County's 840 square miles.

246. In 1983, Hungarian artist Javacheff Christo wrapped pink plastic around 11 islands in Biscayne Bay and dubbed the result *Water Lilies.*

247. In 1972, the Miami Dolphins pulled off the NFL's first perfect season, culminating in a 14-7 win over the Washington Redskins in Super Bowl VII.

248. Babe Ruth's longest homer — 587 feet — was swatted at Tampa's Plant Field in 1919.

249. James Weldon Johnson was born in Jacksonville in 1871, then went on to do just about everything. Besides writing the words to the unofficial African-American National Anthem, "Lift Every Voice and Sing" (his brother John wrote the music), he was principal at Jacksonville's Stanton High, practiced law as the first African-American admitted to the Florida bar and served as diplomat to Venezuela and later Nicaragua. He also was a prolific writer and was instrumental in founding the National Association for the Advancement of Colored People.

250. The last battle of the American Revolution is thought to have been fought off Cape Canaveral on March 10, 1783.

251. Spain ruled Florida for 236 years. The United States will have to wait until 2057 before it can say the same.

252. Besides citrus, Florida is also the nation's foremost producer of watermelons, radishes, snap beans, cucumbers, sweet corn, tomatoes, green peppers and sugar. Let's eat.

253. If Phillip Miller hadn't wanted to sell University of Florida pennants in his Gainesville drugstore in 1907, U of F might now be known as the home of the Fighting Hogs. (Pre-Civil War, the city was named Hogtown). Seems when Miller ordered the pennants, the Michie Company asked which animal to put on the school's emblem. Since the school had no mascot or official emblem, Miller chose the alligator.

254. On Aug. 5, 1997, Freddie Hoffman and his bicycle wheeled into Titusville in plenty of time to take NASA up on its invitation to a VIP view of a *Discovery* shuttle launch. Over the past 30 years, Hoffman has pedaled his bike 1 million miles — far enough for two round trips to the moon — while raising money for Leukemia Society.

255. In 1985, after 16 years of searching, Mel Fisher and his crew of divers found the Spanish galleon *Nuestra Senora de Atocha,* off Key West. Her bounty of gold, silver, emeralds and artifacts was the largest treasure ever recovered.

256. The Golden Age Games, the nation's oldest and Florida's largest senior competition, takes place in Sanford. Events include tennis, synchronized swimming, track and field activities, bicycles racing, checkers, knitting and pinochle. Melding for medals.

257. The Lone Ranger meets Calvin and Hobbs at the International Museum of Cartoon Art and Cartoon Hall of Fame in Boca Raton. The museum, considered the world's first of its kind, features more than 160,000 works by more than 1,000 artists from 50 countries. Exhibits span the cartoon universe, from animated films to historic editorial cartoons by Ben Franklin and Paul Revere.

258. Napoleon's nephew, Achille Murat, was an attorney and judge in Tallahassee. Oui, oui.

259. Because Florida supplied most of the beef to Confederate states during the Civil War, a "cow cavalry" was formed to stop Union forces from killing cattle in the fields. Moo.

260. Henry Flagler's 1,500 room Royal Poinciana Hotel in Palm Beach was so big that bellhops on bicycles delivered messages through the halls.

261. President Warren G. Harding wanted to play golf while vacationing at the Flamingo Hotel in Miami Beach in 1921. So hotel owner Carl Fisher surprised him with a special golf caddy. A baby elephant named Carl II carried the president's clubs. Bet that was a game he never forgot.

262. The nation's first flight school opened in Pensacola in 1914.

263. Way down upon the Yazoo River? That's the way Stephen Foster originally intended to begin "Old Folks at Home". Foster, who never set foot in Florida, picked the Suwannee out of an atlas and cut a syllable off the name so it would fit the music. As a result, the sleepy North Florida river has been called Swannee ever since, and "Old Folks at Home" is Florida's official state song. Even with dialect deleted and "darkies" changed to "brothers" in modern versions, the song continues to draw controversy and a movement is underway to revoke its state title.

264. The official state play, *Cross and Sword*, is performed throughout the summer in St. Augustine.

265. The Civil War Monument in Lynn Haven is one of the few to honor both Confederate and Union soldiers.

266. In 1972, the praying mantis lost its bid for the title of official state insect, a category Florida officials don't seem inclined to honor.

FABULOUS FLORIDA

267. Long before he led the World War II raid on Tokyo, flying ace Jimmy Doolittle set a speed record by flying from Pablo Beach — now called Jacksonville Beach — to San Diego in 22 hours. By the way, Doolittle and his fellow flyers trained for the Tokyo raid at Pensacola's Elgin Air Force Base.

268. Richard C. Bradford of Madison was the first Florida Confederate soldier to die in the Civil War.

269. When Mary Bethune, founder of the school that is now Daytona's Bethune-Cookman College, received an honorary degree from Rollins College in 1949. She was the first African-American woman so honored by a white Southern college.

270. Douglas Dummett of Merritt Island developed the first frost-resistant orange — the Indian River orange. Like many other Merritt Island growers, Dummett was bought out by the government and his land is now part of Kennedy Space Center.

271. Careful. The Everglades is home to the world's largest concentration of sawgrass so sharp soldiers wouldn't pursue Indians who hid in the Everglades during the Seminole Wars.

272. On Feb. 25, 1946, the University of Miami was sold for $927.23 — to the University of Miami. It seems the Coral Gables institution had failed to pay Everglades Drainage District taxes to the tune of $770. According to law, the property had to be advertised for public auction and sold to the highest bidder. Although prime property, no one else bid on the home of the Hurricanes.

273. One of the best freshwater fishing spots in the Panhandle is at Dead Lakes State Recreation Area in Wewahitchka. Hmm, Dead Lakes. No wonder the fish are so easy to catch.

274. In 1986, Bob Martinez was elected Florida's first Hispanic governor.

275. Florida's no. 2 tourist attraction is Busch Gardens.

276. In his 1970 bid for the U.S. Senate, Lawton Chiles walked across Florida to meet and greet would-be constituents. The effort earned him eight years in Washington and the nickname "Walkin' Lawton." After a brief retirement, he was elected Florida's governor in 1990.

277. Near Palatka, he's called Bardin Booger. Around the Space Coast, he's known as the Skunk Ape. While folks can't seem to decide what to call Florida's version of Bigfoot, they all agree on one thing — he smells really bad.

278. Orlando Magic-man, Anfernee Hardaway is best known as Penny, a nickname given him by his grandmother. Well, sort of. She was actually calling him "pretty." To Hardaway's relief, his childhood chums misunderstood what she was saying. Hmmm. Pretty Hardaway. Nah.

FABULOUS FLORIDA

279. Before he became a jazz-world legend, saxophonist Julian "Cannonball" Adderly majored in music at Florida A&M University and went on to teach at Dillard High School for the Performing Arts in Fort Lauderdale.

280. Before the world went blue suede, white bucks were the national shoe, thanks to Jacksonville-born Pat Boone. Besides recording three no. 1 hits, he also made movies, including *State Fair* with Ann Margaret and *April Love* with Shirley Jones.

281. Before it became a ritzy resort, Boca Raton was little more than scenery on the way South. Desperate for attention in 1928, town fathers approved building a wooden camel to stand astride Dixie Highway, hoping to catch the interest of Shriners heading to a convention in Miami. Not to be outdone, the city's Elks raised money to change the camel into an elk. Ten days laterthough, the permit expired and with it died the great Boca camel.

FABULOUS FLORIDA

282. Ex-paratrooper and law student-turned tennis pro Nick Bollettieri opened his Tennis Academy in Bradenton in 1978 "to produce champions." Graduates include Andre Agassi and Andrea Jaeger.

283. The world's first scheduled commercial airplane flight took pilot Tony Jannus from St. Petersburg to Tampa in 1914.

284. Tallahassee claims the lowest temperature ever recorded in the state, a bone-numbing -2° F on Feb.13, 1899.

285. Achtung! The first rocket launched from Cape Canaveral was a German V-2.

286. The most fantastic collection of movie memorabilia in the world is hidden away in a nondescript Orlando warehouse. There are no tours. In fact, you can't get in at any price. This is artifact central for the Planet Hollywood restaurant chain.

287. Go figure. With so many miles of coastline available, one can only wonder why the U.S. Navy Training Center was placed in the middle of the state near Orlando where sailors honed their submarine skills in lakes. The center, the Navy's second largest boot camp, was phased out in 1993.

288. Circus tycoon John Ringling gave his palatial Sarasota home the exotic name, *C d'Zan*, which translated from an obscure Italian dialect means John's house.

289. Jim Morrison of The Doors was born in Melbourne. Although he was there only a short time, local fans considered his house a shrine and spray painted messages on it to the long dead rocker. The practice stopped a few years ago and a new one began — the practice of a plastic surgeon who renovated the building for an office.

290. *USA Today* was born on Sept 15, 1982 in the Cocoa offices of *Florida Today*, now located in Melbourne.

291. Explanations abound when it comes to Shaquille O'Neal's last minute switch from the Magic to the LA Lakers in 1996. But locals believe he simply didn't feel loved. For months, as his agent negotiated a new contract, Shaq insisted he wanted to stay in Orlando. But when the *Orlando Sentinel* took a poll asking if his bigness was worth a proposed $115 million over seven years to re-sign, 91% voted no-way. Days later, Shaq slam dunked Orlando and headed West. Members of the Magic organization, including General Manager John Gabriel, blamed the paper.

292. Bubbly soap opera star Deidre Hall hails from Lake Worth.

293. Central Florida land baron Hamilton Disston paid $1 million for 4 million acres in 1881. Yes, folks, that's 25¢ an acre, the going rate at the time.

294. The town of Penny Farms was founded by department store magnate J.C. Penney as a retirement haven for religious leaders.

295. After years of cranking away, the citizens of Perry finally switched to dial phones on Aug. 31, 1961. They were the last in the state to do so. One ringy-dingy.

296. The Zebra Longwing is the official state butterfly.

297. About 120,000 Cubans fled to South Florida in the Mariel boatlift.

298. If the constant, surgery droning of Disney World's "It's a Small World" ride drives you crazy, blame visitors to the 1964-1965 New York World's fair. The Disney folks tested Small World and the Carousel of Progress there before crating them up and bringing them to Orlando.

299. The state motto is the inventive "In God We Trust."

300. Sally Ride became the first American woman in space on June 1983, aboard the space shuttle *Challenger*. Ride Sally Ride.

301. The infield of Hialiah Race Track is hardly the place for a romantic liaison. Especially when racing season and mating season coincide, as they did after rescheduling in 1972. As a result, the track's 400 resident flamingos stopped mating. In 1981, Angelo Testa, director of track operations, built fake nests and filled them with fake eggs in an attempt to rekindle romantic instincts. Then he had sprinklers installed on top of 100-foot royal palms to add atmosphere — the birds prefer breeding in the rain. When the first new chick hatched a few months later, Testa passed out cigars.

302. Under Spanish rule, the Florida territory included Alabama, Mississippi and Louisiana.

303. Debbie Harry, formerly of the rock group, Blondie, was born in Miami.

304. Pat Palinkas, the Orlando Panther's place kick holder in 1971, was the first woman to play professional football.

FABULOUS FLORIDA

305. Barefootin' became the rage after Dick Pope, Jr., became the first person ever known to water-ski without water-skis on Lake Eloise at Cypress Gardens in 1947.

306. Paul Reubens, AKA Pee Wee Herman, graduated from Sarasota High School in 1970.

307. Early Beatlemania hit its peak when the 10,000 teens crowded Miami International Airport to meet the Fab Four. It was the largest airport turnout of their 1964 tour.

308. Native Floridians make up only about a third of the state's population. Talk about endangered species.

309. To find the largest cattle ranch in the nation (possibly in the world) you'll have to go to Central Florida. Deseret Cattle & Citrus Ranch. Owned by the Mormon Church it covers about 312,000 acres spread across Brevard, Orange and Osceola counties. Hot dogies.

310. Soul man Sam Moore was born in Miami in 1935.

311. After bringing home six Southeastern Conference titles and a first-ever National Championship in his first seven years as University of Florida, head football coach Steve Spurrier got a token of appreciation from the university — a five-year contract worth a cool $2 million a year. That's more than twice the salary of any other collegiate head coach.

312. The endangered Key deer, which lives in the Florida Keys, is only about the size of a large dog.

313. Florida spiny lobsters, "bugs" to scuba divers, have no claws. They do, however, have wanderlust. Their mass migrations, called crawls, have been known to include up to several thousand lobsters walking single file across the ocean floor.

314. Fernandina Beach lays claim to Florida's first and oldest bar, the Palace Saloon.

315. If you hear twin sonic booms, look up quick. That's the sound space shuttles make as they head in for landings at Kennedy Space Center.

316. Florida horse racing began at Hialiah Park on Jan. 15, 1925. About four months later, Florida outlawed gambling. To beat the heat, the track sold postcards with numbers on them. If a number matched the number of a winning horse, the track bought back the postcard for a price that matched the odds. Of course, it was merely coincidence.

317. Florida Southern College has the Wright stuff, seven buildings designed by famed American architect Frank Lloyd Wright — the largest single-site collection of his works in the world. The buildings were mostly constructed by students. How's that for working your way through college?

318. The dish Floridians call swamp cabbage, y'all probably know as heart of palm.

319. Flamingoes are naturally white but are tickled pink by eating shrimp and other pink crustaceans.

320. The official state animal is the Florida panther, an endangered species.

321. A shoot-out in the tiny town of Ocklawaha put an end to Ma Barker's infamous crime spree. It also put an end to Ma Barker. Both Barker and her son, Fred, were killed in a 5 1/2 hour duel with federal agents. Investigators reportedly found 1,500 bullet holes in the lakefront cabin where they were holed up.

322. Ernest Ivy "Boots" Thomas of Monticello was one of the soldiers who raised the American flag on Iwo Jima during World War II. He died in battle five days later, a week before turning 21.

323. When the Collins Bridge finally connected Miami to Miami Beach in 1913, it was hailed as the world's longest wooden bridge.

324. Floridians bought $1 million worth of *Challenger* license plates in the first three months they were available. Proceeds from the plate, which commemorates the 1986 space shuttle *Challenger* explosion, paid for the Astronaut Memorial at SpacePort USA, the Kennedy Space Center Visitors Center.

325. Bob Graham worked at 108 different jobs in two years, before being elected governor. A state senator from Miami Lakes, Graham spent a day each at such jobs as busboy and trash collector during his gubernatorial campaign. He claimed that the experience helped him better understand Floridians' needs. Apparently Floridians agreed. Or maybe they just elected him to give him a steady job.

326. During 1984 and 1985, scientists and students at the Windover Archeological Site in Titusville uncovered four 7,000-year-old skulls — with brains still intact.

327. Actor Pat Hingle was born in Miami in 1924.

FABULOUS FLORIDA

328. Neither rain nor sleet nor snow. But alligators, that's another story. In 1885, the U.S. Post Office established the first mail route between Miami and Palm Beach and E.R. Bradley of Lantana became the first "barefoot mailman." Bradley made the 236-mile, three-day trip between Hypoluxo and Miami once a week, walking partway along the ocean's edge and rowing partway in a small boat. Two years later, the task was taken over by George Charter and Ed Hamilton. The latter was presumed eaten by alligators at Hillsboro inlet while on his appointed rounds. The "barefoot route" was discontinued in 1992.

329. Richard Nixon uttered those immortal words, "I am not a crook," to newspaper editors meeting at Disney World's Contemporary Hotel — located near Fantasyland.

330. Florida students went for free, out-of-state students paid $20 when the state's first university, the University of Florida, opened its doors in 1906.

331. About 5,000 fans turn out each time greyhounds run around Hollywood Greyhound racetrack — at speeds of up to 40 mph.

332. Disney World pays about $23 million a year in taxes. Remember that on April 15. You'll feel better.

333. If U.S. Senator Connie Mack's name sounds familiar, it's because the Cape Coral native was christened after his grandfather, baseball legend Connie Mack, the former owner and manager of the Philadelphia Athletics.

334. Florida's official saltwater mammal is the dolphin, not the porpoise, although many people use the terms interchangeably. Porpoises, also mammals, look more like small whales, lacking the dolphin's signature bottle-nose and bulging forehead. They also lack the dolphins frolicsome nature. So why the confusion? People probably took to using porpoise to distinguish the playful and friendly mammal form the sport fish of the same name. For the same reason, the dolphin fish is most often referred to these days as mahi mahi.

335. When Florida thunderstorms roll in, don't talk on the phone and don't take a shower. Recognized as the lightening capitol of North America, the state reports between six and nine lightening fatalities per year.

336. When settlers first arrived in Florida, Michelangelo was still alive and Shakespeare hadn't been born yet. Sorta puts it in perspective, doesn't it?

337. Thomas Edison made a splash when he installed the state's first home swimming pool at his Ft. Meyers' winter estate.

338. When John Ringling died in 1936, inheritance-haggling relatives couldn't decide on a final resting spot for the circus magnate and his wife, who had died seven years earlier. The bodies were moved twice before they were finally interred by court order on the grounds of the John and Mabel Ringling Museum of Art which the couple built at their Sarasota estate.

FABULOUS FLORIDA

339. The isolation of Cross Creek life cost Marjorie Kinnan Rawlings her marriage, but she loved it too much to leave with her husband, Charles. Instead, she stayed and captured the harshness and beauty of rural Florida life in such novels as *The Yearling* and *Cross Creek*.

340. The record for shortest gubernatorial stint belongs to Wayne Mixon. He held the post for only three days. The former lt. governor just kept the seat warm when Gov. Bob Graham started a new job as U.S. Senator three days before his successor, Bob Martinez, was sworn in.

341. John W. Simonton paid a mere $2,000 for Key West in 1826. The island's former owner, Juan P. Salas of St. Augustine had been granted the island the King of Spain, in 1815.

342. Amelia Earhart was headed around the world but wound up flying into history when she took off from Hialeah on June 1, 1937.

343. The first Florida synagogue, Temple Beth-El, was established in Pensacola in 1874. Shalom.

344. In 1966, Claude Kirk became the first Republican governor since Reconstruction.

345. More UFOs, alien babies and Elvis sightings have been reported in Lantana than anywhere else in the world. Lantana is also the home of *The National Enquirer*.

346. Manatees, the state's official freshwater mammal, are also called sea cows but they're really distant cousins of the elephant.

347. At the turn of the century, children in Jupiter were carried to classes on a lifeboat. The boat, called *Maine*, was once equipment on the famous U.S. battleship by the same name.

348. Always a designing woman, Delta Burke took the beauty pageant route to stardom. She was crowned Miss Florida in 1974, the same year she graduated from Orlando's Colonial High School.

FABULOUS FLORIDA

349. The Allman Brothers moved to Daytona Beach from Tennessee as youngsters and started their classic rock career playing local clubs.

350. For an exciting afternoon among the elite, try the Palm Beach Polo Grounds. Merv Griffin, Joanne Woodward and Paul Newman are frequent visitors. Prince Charles flies in to play. The game is so fast and so demanding that the horses, who are repeatedly called upon to turn on a dime, can only play one, six-minute period, called a chukker. Six chukkers to a game means that players must own six of the expensive, specially trained horses. No wonder it's called the sport of kings.

351. Country singer/songwriter Mel Tillis, these days best known as the father of Pam Tillis, hails from Pahokee. Country singer/songwriter Pam Tillis, also known as the daughter of Mel Tillis, was born in Plant City.

352. For almost 30 years, Yankeetown held the state's record for the most rainfall in a 24-hour period — 38.7 inches, on Sept. 5-6, 1950.

FABULOUS FLORIDA

353. To honor the Nation's 200th birthday in 1976, Melbourne-area school kids raised money to buy an exact, albeit uncracked, replica of the Liberty Bell. Their inspired elders built the Liberty Bell Museum to house it.

354. The annual football game between the University of Florida Gators and the University of Georgia Bulldogs — held in the supposedly neutral city of Jacksonville — is known across the nation as The World's Largest Outdoor Cocktail Party.

355. During the 1930s, Katherine Rawls racked up 33 national titles and broke U.S. and world records in both swimming and diving — becoming the first athlete to win championships in both sports.

356. On June 2, 1912, most of downtown Fort Lauderdale burned to the ground. Shortly thereafter, the town council voted unanimously to form Fort Lauderdale's first volunteer fire department.

357. Stepin' Fetchit, who became the first black movie star with the 1929 film *Hearts in Dixie*, was born in Key West with the name of Theodore Monroe Andrew Perry. His slow-moving, mumble-mouthed characterization — derived from his vaudeville act — set the stereotype for black roles for many years.

358. When Yellow Fever hit South Florida in 1899, Tom Kennedy — known as the Little Doctor — saved many lives. His only credentials — a stint as an Army medic, followed by a job keeping watch over Henry Flagler's legally insane second wife. When the U.S. Bureau of Health charged Kennedy with practicing medicine without a license, a government board not only found him innocent, they also gave him money to get a medical degree.

359. Six-time Grammy nominee Bobby Goldsboro lives on a 120-acre spread in Ocala which produces neither "Honey" nor "Little Green Apples."

360. The United States Croquet Association is based in Palm Beach Gardens. Grab a mallet.

361. Golfer Doug Sanders was four strokes ahead at the end of the 1966 Pensacola Open but didn't win. Swamped by fans, Sanders was so excited that he forgot to sign his score card and was disqualified.

362. Former Democratic presidential nominee William Jennings Bryan was pitching land in Coral Gables when he was called away from his Miami home, Villa Serena, to take on the last and most famous trial of his career, the so-called Scopes monkey trial. He won the case, but died — reportedly of overeating — before he could return to Miami.

363. Florida has produced five Heisman Trophy winners, three of them in the past five years: Danny Wuerffel, University of Florida, 1996; Charlie Ward, Florida State, 1993; and Gino Torretta, University of Miami, 1992.

364. About 500 new sinkholes pop up (make that pop down) in Florida each year.

365. After traveling by train and bullet-proof car, Al "Scarface" Capone moved into his new Miami estate on Easter morning in 1930. Residents protested. The *Miami News* editorialized. The American Legion called for martial law. It took the federal government and some unpaid taxes to move the mobster. In 1931, he was convicted of tax evasion and spent almost eight years in prison before returning to Miami to die of syphilis.

366. The biggest repellent to Florida pioneers was the tiny mosquito, which once traveled in swarms thick enough to smother cattle. Today, the state spends about $80 million annually to keep them in check.

367. Georgia-born, Florida-bred Burt Reynolds has been credited with working harder to bring the movie industry to Florida than anyone else outside the Florida Film Commission. He has shot several movies, including the three-film *Smokey and the Bandit* series, in the Sunshine State.

368. Miami Beach was so run down in the early 1970s that plans were underway to knock it all down and start again. Instead, thanks to the Miami Design Preservation League, about 800 buildings were saved from the wrecking ball and restored, giving Miami Beach new life and the largest collection of art deco architecture in the world.

369. When developer Arthur Galt sold a parcel of land — now Coral Ridge — for $19,389,000, just after World War II, it was the largest private land deal in the U.S. history.

370. Kelly Slater, surfing champ and former *Baywatch* star, learned to shoot the curl in his hometown, Cocoa Beach.

371. Henry Flagler's Palm Beach resort hotel, The Breakers, has burned to the ground twice — once in 1903 and again in 1925. Both times it was rebuilt and still stands today as one of the nation's finest five-star hotels.

372. In 1977, Florida became the first state to allow cameras in the courtroom.

373. Thomas Edison offered to install streetlights along the thoroughfares of his winter home, Fort Meyers, but his neighbors turned him down. They were afraid the lights would keep their cows awake.

374. The longest professional baseball game on record was a 29-inning battle between two Florida State League teams — Miami and St. Pete — held on June 14, 1966.

375. *Three Movements for Orchestra* earned its composer, Miami's Ellen Taaffe Zwilich, the first Pulitzer Prize for musical composition ever awarded to a woman in 1983.

376. John Hersey, author of *Hiroshima* and the Pulitzer Prize-winner, *A Bell for Adano*, lived his final years in Key West where he wrote *Key West Tales* which was published after his death.

377. Buddy Ebsen graduated from Orlando High School in 1926. We-e-e-ll, doggies.

378. And the winner is — it took three days to determine the winner of the first Daytona 500 held in 1959. Finally, after examining film of the finish, officials gave the checkered flag to Lee Petty.

379. Lawrence Kasdan, born in Miami Beach, had to wait 17 years to see his first script, *The Bodyguard*, made into a movie. While he waited, he did a little more writing, including scripts for *The Empire Strikes Back*, *Return of the Jedi, Raiders of the Lost Ark* and *The Big Chill* as well as the screenplay for *The Accidental Tourist*.

380. In 1992, Rep. Jim Bacchus of Orlando won the grand prize in the Voters for Choice Celebrity Cookoff. His entry, Citrus Chili, owed its punched-up flavor to liberal doses of fruit and orange juice. Fellow Democrat Pete Peterson of Tallahassee failed to place with Peterson's Sinkhole Stew, ingredients unknown.

381. Florida's record largemouth bass — the official state freshwater fish — weighed in at 20 pounds, 2 ounces.

382. In 1896, fresh from the triumph of his Civil War tale, *Red Badge of Courage,* Stephen Crane moved to Jacksonville where rumor has it he married a good-natured prostitute. His experiences during a shipwreck off South Florida became fodder for his most famous short story, "The Open Boat."

383. It didn't take long for superstar Emmitt Smith to dazzle University of Florida fans. In his first stint as starter, he broke the school's record for the most yards in a game by racking up 224 against Alabama. By the time the Dallas Cowboys grabbed him as their first-round draft pick after his junior year, he had broken 58 school records in all. But perhaps his greatest accomplishment as a Gator came in 1996, when, after six years of picking up classes as he could during the off-season, he kept a promise to his mother and received his degree.

384. The largest artesian spring system in the world feeds famous Silver Springs, pumping in about 550 million gallons of water daily. At that rate, you could fill your swimming pool in less than two minutes.

385. Tommy Armour was a successful businessman in Scotland when he decided to start a new enterprise in Delray Beach. The business failed but Armour didn't. He went on to become one of America's all-time great golf instructors.

386. Ruth Bryan Owen became the state's first congresswoman in 1928.

387. Palm Beach might be known as Treeless Beach had it not been for a shipwreck in the area. The ship's crew salvaged the cargo, 20,000 coconuts and sold them to locals who planted them.

388. Four poisonous snakes slither through the state: copperhead, coral, cottonmouth and rattlesnake. Snakes alive!

389. We love this game and that game. Florida is home to three professional football teams, two professional basketball teams, two professional hockey teams and one professional baseball team.

FABULOUS FLORIDA

390. Rex Smith, best remembered for co-starring with Linda Ronstadt in the movie version of *Pirates of Penzanze*, was born in Jacksonville in 1956.

391. Hurricanes were nameless before 1953 when the National Weather Service began using women's names to identify them. Women did not find it an honor, so in 1978 the service began alternating male and female names. Thar he or she blows!

392. Hell hath no fury like a pirate scorned. According to legend, the island of Captiva is so named because the pirate Gaspar captured a ship with a Spanish princess aboard and held the young woman captive on the deserted isle. When she failed to warm to his advances, he beheaded her.

393. In 1992, Leanza Cornett of Jacksonville became the first Miss Florida to win the Miss America crown.

394. The International Swimming Hall of Fame is located in Fort Lauderdale. Come see the splashy exhibits.

395. The Fort Lauderdale Museum of Art boasts the nation's largest collection of artwork from the Netherlands as well as the state's largest collection of pre-Columbian and Native-American art.

396. First baseman Steve Garvey was born in Tampa but grew up across the state, near the Dodgers' Spring training camp, Dodgertown, in Vero Beach. By the time he retired from baseball in 1988, he had been named to All-Star Teams 10 times.

397. It's an illusion, of course, but the Ripley's Believe It or Not! museum in Orlando appears to be sliding into a sinkhole. Drop on in to see such novelties as a Mona Lisa made of toast and a vintage Rolls-Royce constructed out of matchsticks.

398. When Elvis Presley performed in Jacksonville on May 13, 1955, the audience got all shook up and rioted following the concert. It is cited as the first such rockin' response to the king, but it was not the last.

399. The Indians named it Pa-hay-okee, which means grassy waters. Author and conservationist Marjory Stoneman Douglas dubbed it river of grass. Officially, it's known as the Florida Everglades. Whatever you call it, there's no other place like it on the entire planet. Only the Southern section of the glades escaped Florida's dredge-and-fill land boom, but it is still world's largest remaining subtropical wilderness.

400. Marineland, just south of St. Augustine, opened in 1938, making it Florida's first and oldest marine park.

401. In the 1830s, salvaging and auctioning cargo from ship-wrecks made Key West the richest city, per capita, in the nation.

402. The National Hurricane Center is located in Coral Gables.

403. The nation's longest bridge, the Florida Key's Seven-Mile Bridge, connects Marathon, also known as Vaca Key, to Sunshine Key.

404. Since 1949, the World Famous Swamp Buggy Races have been run in March, May and October at Naples' Mile O' Mud race track. Presiding over the festivities is a Swamp Buggy Queen, whose crowning each February is followed by a royal mudbath, a dunking in the muckiest part of the raceway.

405. Silver Springs is the home of the *Creature from the Black Lagoon*. At least the movie was shot there, as were the original *Tarzan* flicks, the *Sea Hunt* television series and an episode of *I Spy*.

406. Zellwood is a corny place. It's the home of the Zellwood Corn Festival and the sweetest corn in the state.

407. The curves at Daytona Raceway are so steep cars have to go faster than 60 mph or they'll fall off.

408. The country hit, *Seminole Wind,* by Apopka's Joe Anderson, was a local favorite before the rest of the country discovered it and sent it zooming to No.1.

409. Florida is the only state with its own embassy in Washington D.C. Established by then Governor Bob Graham, the Florida House gives Floridians a place to meet, make hotel and airline reservations and get the low-down on social and governmental doings while visiting the capital.

410. The Mirror Lake Club in St. Petersburg, America's Shuffleboard Capital, has more than 100 shuffleboard courts.

411. About 60% of Florida visitors come to see a mouse. His name is Mickey.

412. Jack Nicklaus, golf's Golden Bear, lives in North Palm Beach where he stays busy designing golf courses.

413. They're not Old Faithful but geysers of sorts can be seen at Blowing Rock Preserve on Jupiter Island. There, a good Northeast wind sends surf blasting through holes in the rocks and high into the air.

414. The first man to cross the Atlantic by air was — nope, not Charles Lindbergh — it was Albert C. Read. Lucky Lindy made the trip solo but the NC-4 bi-plane carrying Read and his five-man crew made the first trans-Atlantic flight eight years earlier. Read's NC-4 can be seen at the U.S. Naval Aviation Museum in Pensacola.

415. Marli Brianna Hughes, a four-year-old lass from Brandon, was chosen from 35,000 hopefuls to be Life cereal's new "Mikey," in August 1997.

416. Daytona's Lyn St. James was the second woman ever to compete in the Indianapolis 500 when she finished 11th in 1992. The only rookie to complete the race, she was the first female to be named Indy Rookie of the Year.

417. Every now and then, a hard-working horse has got to go home for some R and R. Home for the world-famous Lipizzan stallions is Herrmann's Lipizzan Ranch in Myakka City where they relax and rehearse from January through April each year.

418. Frederick Delius became one of Britain's foremost classical composers because he moved to Florida. Unhappy with the prospect of joining his father's wool business, Delius moved to Picolata, intent on growing oranges. Instead he became enthralled with the music African-American residents made each evening and returned to England, inspired to make music his life's work. Many of his compositions contain traces of the songs and spirituals he heard in Picolata.

419. There are only three schools for baseball umpires in the country and Florida has two of them. Don't blame us, though. All really bad calls are made by umpires who studied at that other school in Arizona.

420. Today, Paynes Prairie is flat and grassy, home to wild horses and bison. But a little more than 100 years ago, steamboats crossed the same area, then called Alachua Lake. In 1891, the lake drained into the aquifer so fast that one steamer, the Chakala, was left sitting on dry land. The area has gone from lake to plain several times in recorded history.

421. The Ponce de Leon Hotel in St. Augustine was the first poured-concrete building in the U.S.

422. About 60,000 college students descended on Fort Lauderdale the year after the movie *Where the Boys Are* premiered. Nowadays, Fort Lauderdale isn't all that keen on Spring Breakers, and gladly acknowledges Daytona Beach as Spring Break Capital of the World.

423. On Feb. 15, 1933, a petite Miami housewife saved Franklin Roosevelt's life. Lillian Cross was among the throng welcoming the newly elected president as he rode in an open-air car to Bayfront Park. On the bench next to her was Giuseppe Zangara, an unemployed and disillusioned Italian immigrant. When the bench started wobbling, Cross looked up and saw a gun. Zangara managed to get off five shots as Cross grabbed his arm and twisted it. Four people were injured. Chicago Mayor Anton Cermak was killed in the attack. Cross was unscathed, except for gunpowder marks on her right check.

424. There are only about a dozen white alligators in the world. One of them lives at Silver Springs which also is home for the largest American crocodile in the care of man.

425. The first political candidate to campaign by automobile was Florida gubernatorial-hopeful, Sidney J. Catts in 1916. He won.

426. The first proposed state motto was, "Let Us Alone."

427. Although her writings were influential in the Harlem Renaissance, Eatonville native Zora Neale Hurston was largely forgotten when she died in her hometown in 1960. Several years later, a tombstone was finally placed on her unmarked grave by Alice Walker, author of *The Color Purple*. On it she had engraved, "A genius of the South." Today, Hurston's popularity is again on the rise and Eatonville holds an annual festival to honor her.

428. Western writer Zane Grey was president of the Long Key Fishing Club.

429. Puerto Rican golf great Chi Chi Rodriguez lives in Naples. When he's not on the links, he can be found working with young people and running a program for underprivileged youth.

430. The official state wildflower, the coreopsis, was designated in 1991. Ride the highways and you'll often see these tall daisy-like plants along the road and in Medians. They're used extensively in highway beautification programs because they thrive in direct sun and sandy soil.

431. Tampa's Columbia Restaurant may be the oldest and largest Spanish restaurant in the United States. Ole´.

432. The TV sitcom *I Dream of Jeannie* claimed to take place in Cocoa Beach but other than some stock footage of the Technical Laboratory on nearby Patrick Air Force Base, not a scene was shot there. Still, Jeannie the genie, Barbara Eden, was honored with her own Cocoa Beach street, I Dream of Jeannie Lane. Unfortunately, each time they put the street sign up, it disappears in a blink.

FABULOUS FLORIDA

433. Reading, writing and high-wire walking — Florida State University is the only university in the country with its own top-quality, student–performed circus. Called the Greatest Collegiate Show on Earth, Florida State's Flying High Circus performs the first two weekends in April each year.

434. In 1996, the Jacksonville Jaguars went to the NFL play-offs in only their second season. They share honors with the Carolina Panthers as the first expansion teams ever to go so far so fast.

435. President Harry Truman first came to Key West to shake a cold. He came back to The Little White House for the sun and fun. Even no-nonsense Harry was not immune to the Key West spirit. He once called a "reverse" press conference there and showed up in a tropical shirt, asking all the questions. His daughter is the namesake, not the owner, of the island's Margaret Truman Launderett.

436. Every dog must have his day — in court. On Aug. 19, 1991, Officer Eluo of the Boca Raton Police Department took the stand. His testimony, several loud barks, was so convincing that it took a jury only 15 minutes to convict Rodney Thomas of trying to strangle Officer Eluo, a German shepherd police dog. Thomas had claimed that he was caught unaware and acted in self-defense. Eluo's handler, Officer Rick Barnett, testified that Thomas could not have missed the warnings given. To prove it, Eluo barked loud enough to be heard outside the courtroom and down the halls of the Palm Beach courthouse. Case closed.

437. Daytona doctor Doran Zimmer led a five-year Public Heath Service study which concluded that kissing can cause tooth decay. At least it's not fattening.

438. Rollins College, established in Sanford in 1885, is the states' oldest institution of high learning.

439. The nation's largest egg hunt brought 40,000 children to Manatee in 1991 in search of 120,000 eggs.

440. For 16 years, Ernest Hemingway, the patron saint of Key West, was honored there with the Hemingway Days Festival, a week-long celebration, featuring a look-alike contest, a short story competition, and lots of drinking. In April of 1997, his heirs filed suit. The Key West image of Papa Hemingway was much too rowdy, they said. Besides, they weren't getting a cut of the action. Key West officials said they'd rather call off the festivities than be bullied, and the heirs held their own, milder fest on sleepy Sanibel Island. A counter suit later, the Key West Hemingway Days took place as always. And the battle goes on. Papa would love it.

441. Pitcher Dwight Gooden was born in Tampa in 1964.

442. Lots of bird brains and feathers and bird watchers have spotted about 400 species and subspecies in the state.

443. The Miami Dolphins' first owners in 1965 were lawyer Joe Robbie and entertainer Danny Thomas.

FABULOUS FLORIDA

444. There are two main routes to horse racing's Triple Crown. To complete the Florida route, thoroughbreds must compete in the Flamingo Stakes at Hialeah's Park and two races at Hollywood's Gulfstream Park, the Fountain of Youth and the Florida Derby.

445. Someone left a cake out in the rain and shine. The 275-room Don CeSar Beach Resort in St. Petersburg Beach looks like a colossal, pink wedding cake.

446. Since it was formed in St. Petersburg in 1931, Kids and Kubs has had one strict rule for membership. You must be at least 75 years old to join.

447. One of the biggest bargains in the state can be found at The Ted Williams Museum and Hitters' Hall of Fame near the Citrus Hills. For only $1 for adults, 50¢ for kids, visitors can see films and artifacts from the famed Red Sox star's baseball career as well as memorabilia from his favorite hobby, fishing and his days as a pilot during World War II and the Korean Conflict.

FABULOUS FLORIDA

448. On Dec. 9, 1941, reeling from the bombing of Pearl Harbor, the United States launched a retaliatory attack, and Madison-native Colin Kelly became the first American hero of World War II. Kelly was killed after flying directly into enemy fire to drop three bombs on the battleship *Haruna*. Eleven days letter, President Franklin Roosevelt drafted a letter addressed to the President of the United States in 1956, asking that Kelly's son — then just 18 months old — be admitted to a U.S Military Academy, should he wish to enroll. Colin P. Kelly III graduated from West Point in 1963.

449. Fairchild Tropical Gardens in Coral Gables is the largest tropical botanical garden in the continental U.S. Although Hurricane Andrew destroyed 2,000 trees and damaged much of the garden's 83 acres, hard work and replanting are bringing it back to its original beauty.

450. With 140 boats, Destin has the largest charter boat fleet in the state. It also owns the state record for the biggest blue marlin catch — 980 pounds, 12 ounces.

451. After digging for nine years at Fort Zachary Taylor, a Union stronghold on Key West during the Civil War, Howard England uncovered the largest collection of Civil War cannons ever found. The cannons, along with his other finds, are on display in a museum at Fort Zachary Taylor Park.

452. With an unusual view on marketing, Norman Johnson used an upside-down house to tout his new development, Sunrise Golf Village (known today as the City of Sunrise.) It was quite a sight for 1960 homebuyers who marveled at the model home, where furniture, appliances, even a Pontiac convertible were topsy-turvy.

453. Florida has 4,500 islands larger than 10 acres.

454. Napoleon Bonaparte Broward's resume makes great reading: Governor of Florida, U.S. Senator, Gun Runner. Truth is, it was his illegal but popular activities — supplying arms to Cuban rebels trying to win Cuba's freedom from Spain — that gained him fame and started his political career.

FABULOUS FLORIDA

455. Florida became the 27th state on March 3, 1845.

456. Beloved for his down-home, play-by-plays, Red Barber was the voice of the New York Dodgers and Yankees for many years. Barber grew up in Sanford and honed his craft at the University of Florida. After retiring to Tallahassee, he produced a popular weekly commentary for National Public Radio. The microphone Barber used at U of F is now on exhibit at the National Baseball Hall of Fame in Cooperstown, NY.

457. The Orange County town of Christmas got its name from Fort Christmas which was established on Christmas Day in 1837 and abandoned three months later. The town is tiny but its post office business is huge. Thousands of holiday cards are bundled and sent there each year to receive a genuine Christmas postmark. The movie, *Ernest Saves Christmas*, was filmed in Florida but had nothing to do with this town.

458. Sanford is the Celery Capital of the World. Crunch.

459. Geronimo, the famous Apache chief, was held prisoner at
Ft. Pickens on Pensacola's Santa Rosa Island from
October 1886 to May 1888 before being moved to Fort
Sill in Oklahoma where he died. In true Florida fashion,
he became a tourist attraction. The curious were brought
in by the boatload.

FABULOUS FLORIDA

SELECTED REFERENCES

Awesome Almanac Florida, Cima Star & Jean F. Blashfield. B&B Publishing, 1994.

Baseball in Florida, Kevin M. McCarthy, Pineapple Press, 1996

Destination Florida Online, various articles, Knight-Ridder and The Tribue Co.

The Everglades: River of Grass, Marjory Stoneman Douglas, Pineapple Press, Special Anniversary Edition, 1997

Florida Department of Tourism, various publications.

Florida Fun Facts, Eliot Kleinberg, Pineapple Press, 1995.

FABULOUS FLORIDA

Florida Fun Facts Online, Florida Department of State, 1997

Florida Off the Beaten Path: A Guide to Unique Places, Bill and Diana Gleasner, Globe Pequot Press, 1993

Florida Place Names, Allen Morris, University of Miami Press, 1974.

Florida: The Strange And The Curious, Lloyd Turner Nightengale, Vantage Press, 1970.

Florida Today, various issues

Glimpses of South Florida History, Stuart McIver, Florida Flair Books, 1988.

A Guide To Florida's Historic Markers, Bicentennial Commission of Florida, Department of State, Division of Archives, History and Record Management, 1972.

FABULOUS FLORIDA

Hidden Florida: The Adventurer's Guide, Third Edition, Stacy Ritz, Candace Leslie, Marty Olmstead and Chelle Koster Walton, Edited by Ray Riegert, Ulysses Press, 1993

Hollywood East: Florida's Fabulous Flicks, James Ponti, Tribune Publishing, 1992.

Insight Guides: Florida, Edited by Paul Zach, APA Productions, 1982.

Miami Herald, various issues

Orlando Sentinel, various issues

Things I Betcha Didn't Know About Florida! Grayson Darr, Valkyrie Press, 1977.

A Treasury of Florida Tales, Webb Garrison, Rutledge Hill Press, 1989

FABULOUS FLORIDA

Unique Florida: A Guide to the State's Quirks, Charisma, and Character. Sarah Lovett, John Muir Publications, 1993.

Zora! Zora Neale Hurston: A Woman and Her Community. Edited by N.Y. Nathiri, Orlando Sentinel Communication Co., 1991

Premium gift books from PREMIUM PRESS AMERICA include:

I'LL BE DOGGONE

CATS OUT OF THE BAG

STOCK CAR TRIVIA

STOCK CAR GAMES

STOCK CAR DRIVERS & TRACKS

STOCK CAR LEGENDS

GREAT AMERICAN CIVIL WAR

GREAT AMERICAN COUNTRY MUSIC

GREAT AMERICAN GOLF

GREAT AMERICAN STOCK CAR RACING

ANGELS EVERYWHERE

MILLENNIUM MADNESS

ABSOLUTELY ALABAMA

AMAZING ARKANSAS

FABULOUS FLORIDA

GORGEOUS GEORGIA

SENSATIONAL SOUTH CAROLINA

TERRIFIC TENNESSEE

VINTAGE VIRGINIA

TITANIC TRIVIA

LEONARDO—TEEN IDOL

BILL DANCES FISHING TIPS

DREAM CATCHERS

THE REDNECK GUIDE TO WINE
  SNOBBERY

PREMIUM PRESS AMERICA routinely updates existing titles and frequently adds new topics to its growing line of premium gift books. Books are distributed though gift and specialty shops, and bookstores nationwide. If, for any reason, books are not available in your area, please contact the local distributor listed above or contact the Publisher direct by calling 1-800-891-7323. To see our complete backlist and current books, you can visit our website at www.premiumpress.com. Thank you.

Great Reading. Premium Gifts.